Amazing Americans: Abigail Adams

Jennifer Overend Prior, Ph.D.

Consultants

Shelley Scudder
Gifted Education Teacher
Broward County Schools

Caryn Williams, M.S.Ed.
Madison County Schools
Huntsville, AL

Publishing Credits

Conni Medina, M.A.Ed., *Managing Editor*
Lee Aucoin, *Creative Director*
Torrey Maloof, *Editor*
Marissa Rodriguez, *Designer*
Stephanie Reid, *Photo Editor*
Rachelle Cracchiolo, M.S.Ed., *Publisher*

Image Credits: Cover, pp. 1, 6-7, 10–11, 12, 14, 14–15, 16, 18, 19, 20, 21, 32 The Granger Collection; p. 9 Bridgeman Art Library; p. 5 Corbis; p. 26 Getty Images; p. 8 The Library of Congress [LC-USZ62-96042]; p. 13 The Library of Congress [LC-USZC4-12540]; pp.20–21 The Library of Congress [LC-DIG-ppmsca-09502]; p. 22 The Library of Congress [LC-DIG-highsm-14860]; p. 23(left) The Library of Congress [LC-USZC4-2474]; p. 25 The Library of Congress [LOC-USZ62-55283]; p. 7 Massachusetts Historical Society; pp. 3, 24, 27 Nancy Carter/North Wind Picture Archives; p. 15 Newscom; p. 29 Ruby Mae Elmore; p. 23(right) Stephanie Reid; p. 17 The White House Historical Association; p. 28 Wendy Jo Lippman; p. 6 Mather Brown 1788, back cover Public Domain/Wikimedia; All other images from Shutterstock.

Teacher Created Materials
5301 Oceanus Drive
Huntington Beach, CA 92649-1030
http://www.tcmpub.com

ISBN 978-1-4333-7004-5

Table of Contents

This is the home where Abigail was born.

Young Abigail

Abigail Adams was a brave woman. She was not afraid to speak her mind. She was born on November 11, 1744, in Weymouth (WEY-muhth), Massachusetts (mas-uh-CHOO-sits). She was the second of five kids.

This is young Abigail.

Abigail's mother was caring. She helped needy families. Abigail's father was a pastor. He was in charge of a church. Back then, many schools only allowed boys to attend. So, Abigail's mother taught her and her sisters at home. Abigail loved to learn. She read many of her father's books.

Love Letters

Abigail met John Adams in 1759. They spent many hours together, but they also wrote each other many love letters. Abigail's mother did not like John. She did not think he was good enough for Abigail.

John Adams

Pen Names

In their letters, Abigail and John used pen names. Abigail was Diana, after the Roman goddess of the moon. John was Lysander (lahy-SAN-der), after the Spartan war hero.

This is Harvard college in 1767.

John graduated from Harvard College. He worked hard as a lawyer. He helped people in court. He saved his money. Soon, Abigail's mother changed her mind. Abigail and John were married on October 25, 1764.

[AA to JA] [4 Dec. 1796] XXXI 152

My Dearest Friend Quincy Decbr 4th 1796

The weather has been & held so uncommonly cold ever since you left me, that I had no expectation of getting a line from you untill you reachd N York. but that line I have not yet received. and by this time I presume you have reachd the city of Sedition, the Hot bed of France. I wrote you this day week, and inclosed to you our Sons Letters, Genll Lincoln & mrs Lincoln dined with me yesterday on their return from Boston & left me the papers. Centinal Mercury & Chronical, all of them are nearly filld with Elects Vote, and consequently leave little room for Speculation, an extract of a Letter in the Chronical from Virginna ... tells us that mr Jefferson will have an unanimous vote there. the majority of the Federal Ticket is given by the same paper in Pensylvania, by which I presume they have lost hopes of an alteration. Elects Vote does not create any great allarm here the Chronical as might be expected, shakes it over us as the rod in pickle: as an event to have been looked for after the audacious treaty we had the assurance to make with great Britain, "Where is the American who does not behold the Salvation of America, included in the protection the French republick, but as if Heaven intended to chastise the measures of our Government in not considering that the cause of France and America was one

This is one of Abigail's letters to John.

More Letters

Abigail and John moved to a farmhouse in Braintree, Massachusetts. Their family began to grow. They had a daughter named Abigail in 1765. John Quincy was born in 1767. The next year, Susanna was born. Later, they had two more sons, Charles and Thomas.

This is Abigail and John's farmhouse in Braintree.

John went to Philadelphia (fil-uh-DEL-fee-uh) in 1774 to meet with the Continental (kon-tn-EN-tl) Congress (KONG-gris). It was a meeting of leaders from the 13 **colonies** (KOL-uh-neez). The people who lived there were called **colonists** (KOL-uh-nists). The colonists were not happy about being ruled by Great Britain. They wanted to make their own laws.

These are leaders at the Continental Congress.

In 1776, John joined a team to write the Declaration of **Independence** (in-di-PEN-duhns). It was a **document** (DOK-yuh-muhnt) that said why the colonies wanted to be free from Great Britain. John wrote to Abigail during this time. He told her about his meetings and asked her for advice.

The colonists fight British soldiers.

In a letter to John, Abigail wrote to "remember the ladies." She wanted laws that made things fair for women. She wanted these laws in the document. But many people did not agree with her. The laws were not added to the Declaration of Independence.

The American Revolution

The American Revolution (rev-uh-LOO-shuhn) started in 1775. It was a war between the colonies and Great Britain. The colonists were fighting for their freedom.

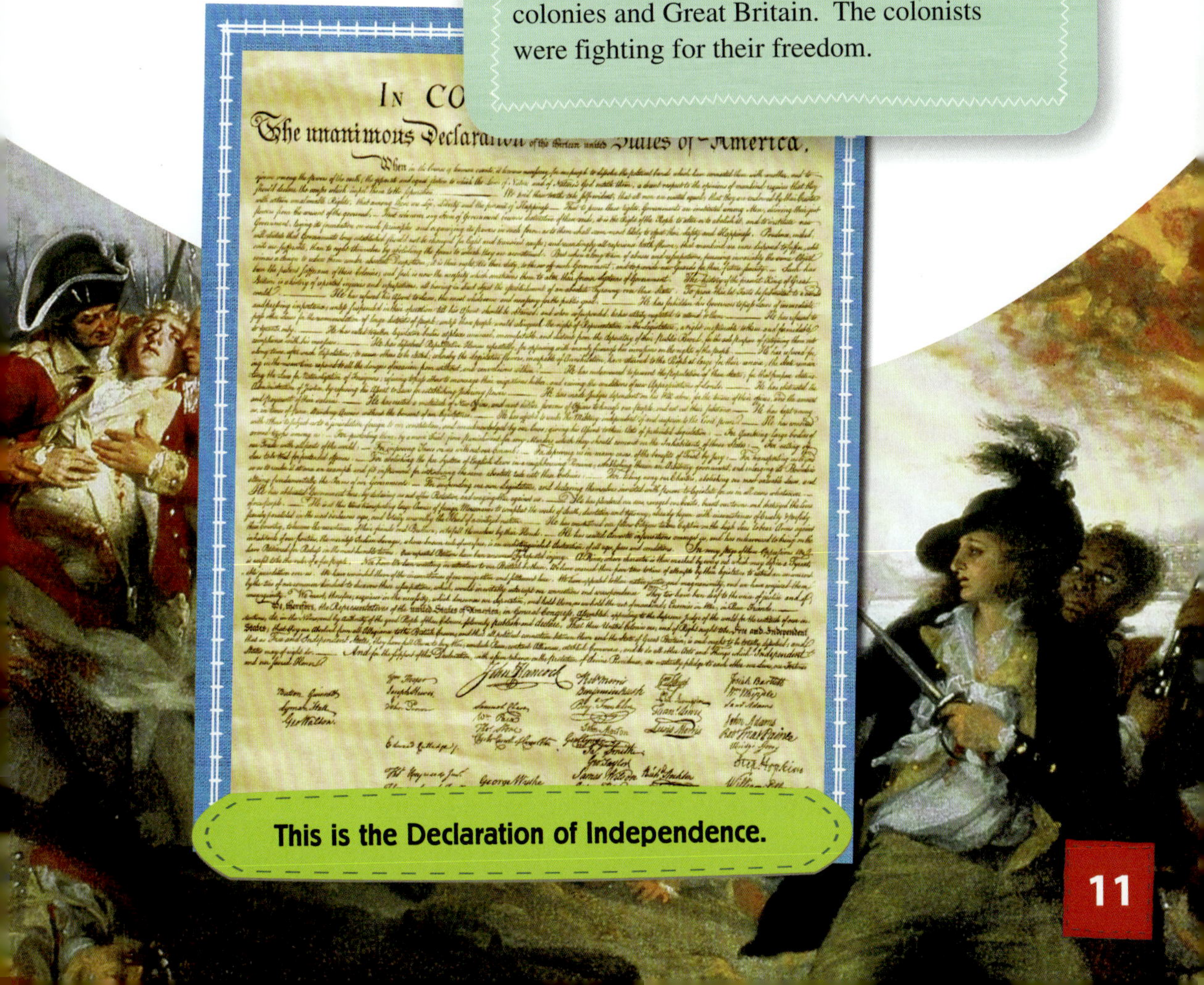

This is the Declaration of Independence.

Important Jobs

While John was away, Abigail worked for the local **government** (GUHV-ern-muhnt). She worked for the Massachusetts Colony General Court. She was a judge (JUHJ) of **Tory** ladies. Her job was to question women in town who might be loyal to Britain. She did not want anyone to get in the way of independence.

Long Live the King!

A colonist who supported Great Britain and the king was often called a Tory.

These boys are making fun of a Tory.

This job gave Abigail a way to voice her own thoughts. She talked about **politics** and what she believed. John was very proud of her important job.

This is the Old State House in Boston. It was the center of politics in the area.

The American Revolution ended in 1783. The colonies were free! Abigail spent the next four years with John in France and England. He was working as a **diplomat**. A diplomat is a person who represents his or her country's government in another country.

This is a French travel guide that was owned by John Adams. He used this while he was in France.

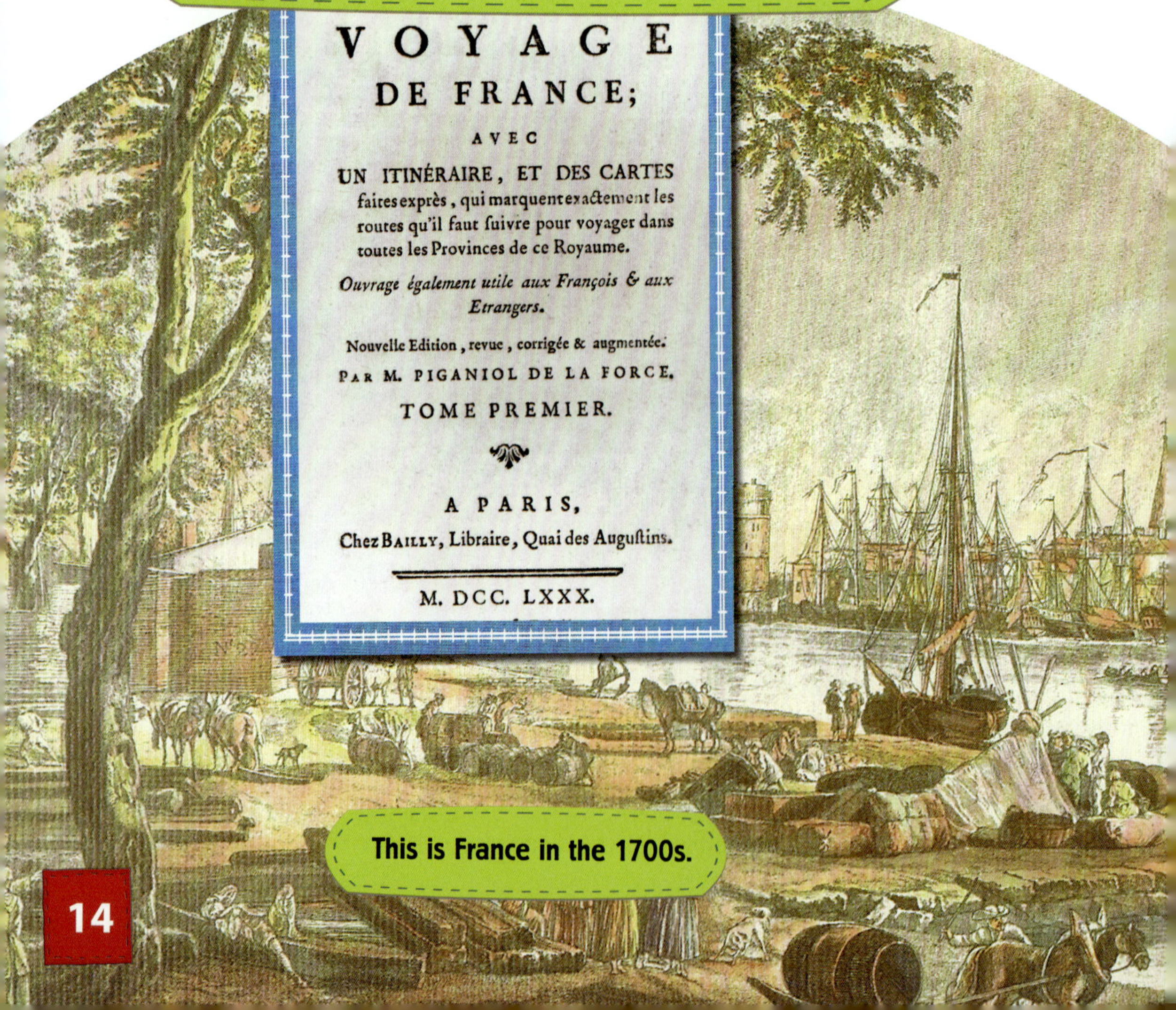

VOYAGE

DE FRANCE;

AVEC

UN ITINÉRAIRE, ET DES CARTES faites exprès, qui marquent exactement les routes qu'il faut ſuivre pour voyager dans toutes les Provinces de ce Royaume.

Ouvrage également utile aux François & aux Etrangers.

Nouvelle Edition, revue, corrigée & augmentée.

PAR M. PIGANIOL DE LA FORCE.

TOME PREMIER.

A PARIS,

Chez BAILLY, Libraire, Quai des Auguſtins.

M. DCC. LXXX.

This is France in the 1700s.

Being the wife of a diplomat kept her busy. Abigail met many important people. She entertained them and learned about them. She represented her country with pride and skill.

This is Abigail in 1785.

This house in Philadelphia is where Abigail and John lived while he was president.

First Lady

In 1788, Abigail and John moved back to Braintree. The next year, John was elected vice president of the United States. *Elected* means that people chose him by voting. He was vice president from 1789 to 1797. Then, he was elected president in 1797. This made Abigail the First Lady.

The White House

Abigail and John lived in the newly-built White House for the last four months of his time as president.

This is how the White House looked when Abigail lived there.

Abigail had many duties as the First Lady. She went to public events. She met with important people. She held fancy dinners and parties.

As First Lady, Abigail was not afraid to speak her mind. She stood up for John when people spoke badly about him. Some people did not like that Abigail talked about politics. But she kept saying what she thought.

This statue honors Abigail because she stood up for her beliefs.

Many people knew that John asked Abigail for advice. They called her "Mrs. President." Even so, he did not always do as she wished. But that did not stop Abigail. She kept speaking up.

This is a portrait of Abigail.

This is the President's House in 1817.

John Quincy Adams

The year 1800 was full of ups and downs for Abigail and John. They were happy to be the first to live in the White House. At the time, it was called the President's House. They were also very proud of their son John Quincy. He was doing well in politics. He was a successful (suhk-SES-fuhl) diplomat.

Charles Adams

Abigail and John were not as happy later in the year. John lost the election (ih-LEK-shuhn) to Thomas Jefferson. His days as president would soon be over. Then in December, their son Charles died. He was only 30 years old.

After the White House

In March 1801, Abigail and John moved to Quincy, Massachusetts. Abigail spent her time taking care of their home. She also spent time with their kids and grandkids.

This is Abigail and John's home in Quincy.

Abigail kept writing. She was still very interested in politics. She wrote letters to Thomas Jefferson when he was president. She also wrote to Dolley Madison when Dolley was First Lady.

During this time, Abigail also focused on her son John Quincy. She was very proud of him. He had been a diplomat in many countries. He also became secretary of state.

John Quincy works at the House of Representatives.

Abigail wrote her son letters. She gave him advice. Sadly, Abigail died on October 28, 1818. She never got to see her son become president of the United States in 1825.

This is John Quincy Adams in 1815.

An Inspiration

Abigail's grandson **published** her letters in 1848. It had been 30 years since her death. Her letters tell about an important time in history. They show her love for her family. They show her love for her country.

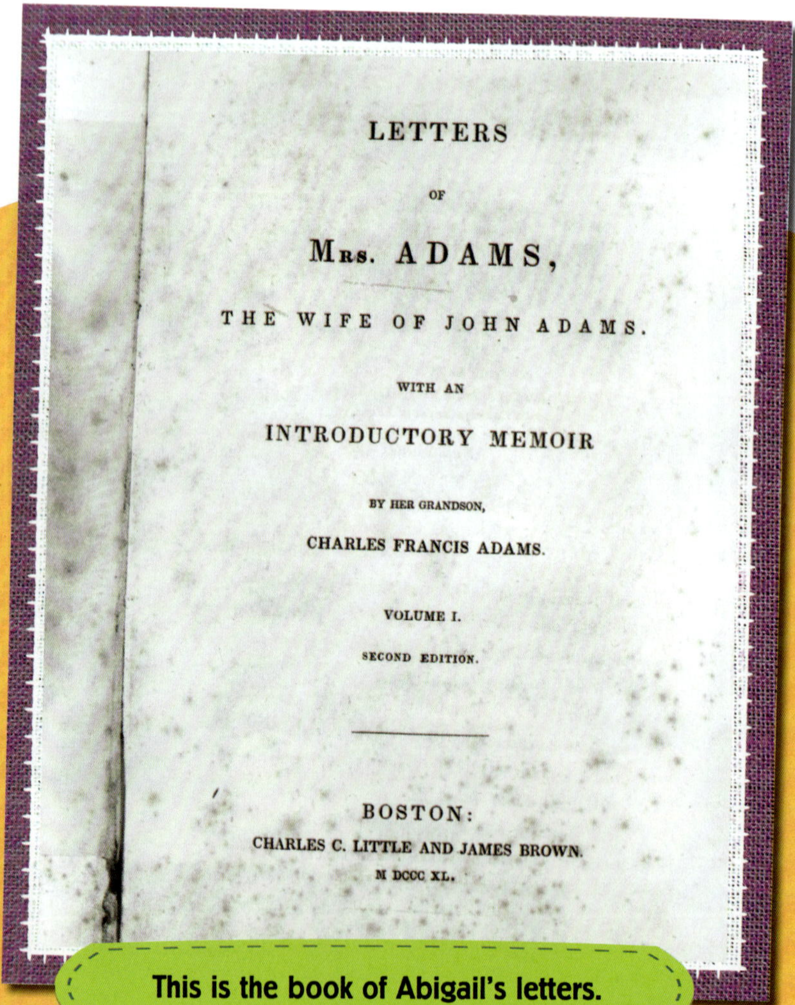

LETTERS

OF

Mrs. ADAMS,

THE WIFE OF JOHN ADAMS.

WITH AN

INTRODUCTORY MEMOIR

BY HER GRANDSON,

CHARLES FRANCIS ADAMS.

VOLUME I.

SECOND EDITION.

BOSTON:

CHARLES C. LITTLE AND JAMES BROWN.

M DCCC XL.

This is the book of Abigail's letters.

Abigail was a brave and strong woman. She was not afraid to speak her mind. She stood up for her beliefs. Abigail continues to be an **inspiration** to others.

This statue shows Abigail and John Quincy.

Amazing Americans Today

Abigail Adams was an amazing American. She stood up for what she believed.

Today, there are many amazing Americans. They help people, too.

This is Ruby Mae and her Aunt Wendy. Wendy is a fire captain. She helps kids learn that fires are dangerous.

Ask It!

Ask an adult to help you find an amazing American in your town. Interview the person. Find out what he or she does to make your town a better place.

Ruby Mae drew this picture of her Aunt Wendy.

Glossary

colonies—areas ruled by a country far away

colonists—people living in an area that is ruled by another country

diplomat—a person who represents his or her country's government while in another country

document—an official paper that gives information about something

government—a group of leaders who make choices for a country

independence—freedom to make decisions

inspiration—something that makes someone want to do something

politics—having to do with government

published—prepared and produced a book for sale

Tory—a person who was loyal to Great Britain in colonial days

Index

Your Turn!

Who Is Your Inspiration?

This photo shows a statue of Abigail Adams. She is an inspiration to many people.

Who is your inspiration? Maybe it is a parent or teacher. Tell that person why he or she is an inspiration to you.